SPOKEN WORD

Told By a Closed Mouth

SPOKEN WORD
Told By a Closed Mouth

By Ramon Bonner

Published by

MIDNIGHT EXPRESS BOOKS

SPOKEN WORD
Told By a Closed Mouth

2012 Ramon Bonner

ISBN-10: 0989463028

ISBN-13: 978-0-9894630-2-7

Published by
MIDNIGHT EXPRESS BOOKS
POBox 69
Berryville AR 72616
(870) 210-3772
MEBooks1@yahoo.com

SPOKEN WORD
Told By a Closed Mouth

By Ramon Bonner

Dedication

For all the accomplishments that I have achieved and for all the ones that I am still reaching for, I dedicate this book to the one woman, the one person in my life that has kept pushing and motivating me to be successful. To this woman, I thank you! For your love, I thank you! For my life, I thank you and will always love you!

To my mother Ramona Booth

Contents

A DREAM

When I close my eyes at
night, I think of you
I think about how our
love is true
I think how much you
mean to me and I to you
I think how empty my
heart was away from you
A dream that's dreamed
with a broken heart
Those are the ones that
set us apart
Some dream about what
could've been
Others about what could
be
Instead of what is.

Live in the moment;
Forget the past
And be surprised by the
future!

Ramon Bonner

A QUOTE FOR LOVE

I trust in my ability to make
life changes
Looking and searching for
love in all the wrong places
Love at first site
Thought it was that love of
truth
Which later down the road
that true turned to lies
Yes we are not getting
younger, in fact, time is
passing
Strive for what
grandparents have, that
love forever lasting!

BEFORE WE MET

I had all these thoughts
about you
as my eyes were reduced to
just a picture
Since I met you in person
Your beauty is so much
clearer
Your eyes tells a story full
of emotions that warms me
Your accent is so sexy like
gravity it pulls me
The sweet smile from my
sweet lady it holds me
Although my sweet lady is
his sweet lady,
I shall try not to intervene
Understand you had a part
of my heart
(Although it could be just a
crush)
Since the moment your
picture came across my
screen.

BEST FRIEND

Me and my best friend, we
walk hand and hand
Like birds of a feather that
flocks together, my best
friend and I now and
forever, through pain and
terror, we stand together in
any weather; that's my best
friend!
If she plummets, ill seize
her with no reluctance ere
perceiving she's falling
We can conversate about
nothing, like it's something
in such a way that, although
the conversation is
irrelevant, the passion and
sincerity makes it relevant
to the outsiders not embody
in the union of this

friendship; THAT'S MY
BESTFRIEND
(sigh)(but)
Truth is, I'm in love with
my best friend!
I'm absolutely head over
hills, I DO til death do us
part,
First thing I see when I
wake, last thing I kiss
before I rest
Bullet through my heart to
keep her alive; in love with
my BESTFRIEND!
I mean this is not
something I envisioned
happing!
In-fact, I enjoy being her
BESTFRIEND,
Her shoulder to cry on
Her ear to vent to
Her pillow to rest her head
on when she's down;

I enjoy being that of all she
needs in a friend! But
My shoulder then became
too wet
My ears became too sad
My chest became too
familiar for the wrong
reason; which made my
heart do some thinking, and
my mind does some
wondering
I, I should be who prevents
her from shedding all the
tears
I, I should be her MAN!
(YES) but how?
How do I let her know?
How do I let her know that
I'm who she should be
with?
How do I let her into that
part of my heart that's more
than just friends without

suppressing the beautiful
essence between us two?
I could tell her! (Yeah, ha)
naw, then she'll say
"OH! Um I just don't like
you like that! But I do hope
things don't change
between us!"
Yeah, like I can just be with
her every day, hold her
when she's down, or just
joke and laugh with her
without feeling like I
swallowed a 100 pound
bolder
Naw, from that point on, I
would just feel empty
Like I lost my best friend.
Although I'm staring right
at her
As if nothing would feel
right or complete without
knowing she's my woman

My heart
My life
My world (DAMN!)
Naw, on second thought I'll
keep it to myself!
I can deal with me having
feelings for my best friend
and not knowing hers; but
I can't deal with her not
sharing the same feelings if
she knows!
So, some things are just
better left unsaid!
So, as I close my eyes at
night, I'll do so with a
smile on my face;
Cause for all I know the
smiles, laughs, and hugs we
shared today came from the
same place in her heart as
in mines!
So, in those moments
shared it is in-fact like we

were more than just

BESTFRIENDS!
AT LEAST IN MY
WORLD!

BLIND LOVE

Love is blind, it don't see
weight
or race and I don't have the
time to settle for second
place
I'm Romeo looking for
Juliet
and if I say that I love her
I be damn if my family say
I can't
black
white
Dominican
Mexican
or Asian
either one is fine with me
see love is blind and I'm
Ray Charles
looking for my queen B by
putting my hand around her
arm
she can be ugly to you but
fine to me
only love knows true
beauty
and true beauty is more
than just skin deep

BLIND STARES OF A MILLION EYES

Yeah! I know who I am,
inside and out
In-Fact!, I know everything
that makes me work, but
blind stares of a million
eyes say; I'm portraying to
be someone who I'm not
See now deception is just
another part of the devils
game; but deceive me not
and I shall not deceive
those along the way of the
path of success and
greatness I intend to seek

I mean yeah, I do move to a
different beat that of no one
else's drum, but these blind
stares of a million eyes
continue to play but they all
still hearing just one thumb
So as along as those blind
stares of those million eyes
continue to be confined to
the small coordinated box
that lives inside, that give
them the reason to see me
only as the way they
perceive me;
Then I WILL NOT
welcome their views to
allow me to commit
miscues in which would
ultimately veer me down
another direction in which I
do not plan to take

See you can be successful

and you can be great;
although the world may
perceive you in a different
light, just do you and prove
people wrong!
(The meaning behind
"blind stares of a million
eyes")
Anything that you do in the
world rather you set out to
better yourself, do good in
the world, or whatever;
there are always people
watching you. People are
always waiting for you to
mess up and fail. If you're
doing good for yourself,
people will never see that
so basically they're blind to
all the good that you do. So
in conclusion don't do
things to get appreciation,
do things because it feels

right and good to you!!

CAN I

Can I lay your body down
Kiss your body slow
whisper in your ear
rub your body head to toe
can I love you down, let me
love you down
I'll run a bubble bath
take off your clothes
slow jams playing, candles
lit
while you soak
can I love you down, let me
love you down
I'll rub ice down your neck
then move to your breast
down to your belly and you
know
What's next

can I love you down, let me
love you down
It's getting hot in here
our bodies soaking wet
your skin next to mine
while I'm
licking down your neck
can I love you down, baby
let me
love you down

DIFFERENT

I was a boy
That grew into a man

Did you hear that, listen
closely; I said
I stand here today as the
man I am, because of who I
was as a boy
(damn) now I think about
it, that was easy for me to
say
It continue to be easy every
minute of every day to
wake in the morning look
in the mirror and say I
WAS A BOY, THAT
GREW INTO A MAN
For some others it doesn't
come that way

See I understood from a
boy to a teenager, to a man
that that's what I was
becoming
A MAN!
I didn't have adults look at
me as a child with blank
looks and frowns that when
playing dress up with my
siblings instead of jeans I
would wear a gown
Because I knew back then I
was a boy
Adults steady try to teach
kids right from wrong,
wrong from right and think
that's gonna make their
child turn out alright
(yeah) until that little boy
comes home drenched from
all of the pain and hurt that
had drained from the very
eyes that had looked up at

his parents as they taught him right from wrong, right being never to judge a person by the color of their skin but they was too scared to prepare him for what could happen being different to where he won't fit in now they have to answer the questions from beginning to end like "what makes me different mom?" "Why don't I have friends?" "Is it because I like things that girls like and I'm a boy?" "Why am I a boy then?" WAIT!! See! It was easy for me to say I was boy simply because I never had thoughts that told me different So for the man who never had thoughts so different that sits next to whom thinks no different that sits across from a man that looks, walks, talk, and acts different; is that of what's being said "DIFFERENT" and they don't understand So how can a person who never understood the meaning of being different understand and pass judgment on one that is "gay" TELL ME! If you judge those who are gay, then you're actually judging those who are different and in this world no two persons are the

Spoken Word

same therefore we are all
different, which means in
all actuality those who are
gay are normal then you
would actually be making
fun of yourselves.

I admit there was a time, I
as a straight man, stood
blind to the gays
Never had a problem with
people being different my
mind was just closed to
understanding their ways
Naïve as a boy as I laughed
and pointed, not a care in
the world as a teenager
pretending things went
unnoticed
But as I said before I WAS
A BOY, THAT GREW
INTO A MAN
A man that now see, just by

observing like a bird from a
tree, what its like to be
different, or gay so to
speak!
No one chose to be
different
So why can't we all just be
the same
Being different is not a
curse
its unique like a name!

I was a boy
You was a boy
That grew into men!

*Dedicated to Demario
Watson & LaTrice
Crawford*

EMOTIONS

For those who loves me
For those who don't
For those I care about
For those I won't
My heart is here where it
lies for that special one who
loves my soul and mind
My tears fall like rain that
won't be caught by a
window pane
On the floor is a puddle of
me to be stepped over
through, or on
As long as I stay a real man
and let my hurt emotions
show
What once was a puddle of
me will be mopped up and
dried

One day by that woman
who will pick me up
Dust me off and love my
heart
Soul, and Mind!

EVERY DAY YOU'RE SPECIAL

I kiss you on your right
cheek
To let you know ill always
be by your side.
I kiss you on your left
cheek
To let you know I'm your
best friend
I kiss you on your forehead
So you know with me
you're safe
I kiss you on the tip of your
nose
Just because you giggle and

smile in that sexy way
I kiss you on your lips
Then tell you "I'm yours
only, and I'm here to stay".

Let your girl know how
special she is to you every
day in any way!

HOW IN LOVE ARE YOU

How in love are/or were
you
If the one you supposedly
loved is so quickly easily
replaced?
How down are/or were you
If after one real fight you
were easily gone?
How true are/ or were you
If a simple " I hope u have
a great day" is hard to
believe?
The words "I love you" are
so easy to say and easily
said
Those same easy words are

the hardest to hit
The hardest to lose
The hardest to return!

Love is not a game! Pick
and choose wisely who u
let get that part of you!

IF TODAY ENDED

If today suddenly ended so
soon, or tomorrow at noon
I could say my life was
complete if it ended with
me next to you
At the moment I can't say
that I'm in love with or by
you
At this moment I can say I
fell in-like from the
moment my eyes met you
Blind to the world
Def to all sound
Struck by your beauty the
rest can be left out
Though times is uncertain
and it could stop in a blink

My love can't tell time so
the rest is obsolete

IN THE MIND of a CHILD

In the mind of a child
Those who are closest to
them are their heroes
In the mind of a child
There are no comic books,
power rangers no, none of
that
Just those who been there
since day one
In the mind of a child
Anything they are told by
their heroes they believe
not because they know no
better, but because of who
that speaks
In the mind of one child

Who lie alone in his bed
hears a knock as he falls
asleep
He Feels confused as he
was told to let the knocks
that awoken him sooth
He hears no knocks and
sees a hero that no longer
belonged come furiously
down the hall
In the eyes of one child
Sees the hero that don't
belongs grab a close love
one and do her wrong
He opens the door and sees
his hero doing actions that
he as a child did not
understand yet, but
understood his love one
was trying to run away
from.
Through the ears of one
child

Spoken Word

Hears the screams, pain,
and cries of his loved one
In the heart of one child
He feels hurt, pain, and
anger
In the soul of one child
He feels worthless as he
listened but too young to
physically do anything
In the mind of one child
He felt like killing his hero
In the mind of one child
That child was me. DAMN!

INTENTIONS

People always say that
guy's intentions with a
female are bad from the
start.
Well I've known you for a
while now, and my
intentions always been to
have you in my life no
matter what.
Now as we gotten older and
became who we are as
adults,
I admit that my intentions
have changed. I am no
longer content with you just
being in my life, but
now I am driven to MAKE
YOU my life!
Although yesterday is
obsolete, and today can be
confined;

the future is the goal I reach
for, the one where you
would be the prize.
So if these are bad
intentions then I guess i am
just one of the guys, but
This guy's aspirations
would be devoted to
keeping you with a smile,
your heart filled with bliss
and start and ending each
day with a kiss!
Now I see the time for us is
not now,
No, no need to be in a rush.
Although life is on a time
clock, ill max mines out
twice reason being,
I know that when it comes
down to it, and the time is
right;
I DO, I DO, I DO when I'm
asked if I take you as my
wife!

LIGHT OF LOVE

When you're away there's
darkness
when you're with me
there's light
I may appear smiling and
happy to most but when
I'm with you its true
Although between us
there's miles,
There's states
There's rivers and lakes
I'll run the distance
I'll swim the length if it
means I can see your face
Like, lust, and love
Have completely different
meanings
I can like you for a second
I can lust for you for a
moment
I can love you forever
So whatever is between us
can't keep me in the dark
and you from sight
Because I would do
anything to get to you
My light!

Love Story

What's a love story if the
story of love isn't true?
Too many, not just a few
have something they call
love but constantly bring in
outside lust to
accommodate
insecurity, mixed feelings,
and the inability to grow up
and understand
that what you have is
special and life changing
that nothing else outside
your bond between your
lover/best-friend/and your
heart (your woman/man)
MATTERS!

LOVE

Love is more than just
putting your lips together
saying a word or some
letters.

L.O.V.E is a feeling that
should settle that has a
meaning when you and I
are together
The eye gazing, holding
hands, the conversations
with no words that still
have you showing that
smile that lights up my
world, you know what I'm
saying,
the child play, love hitting,
better known as love taps,
that turns into love kisses

ending in sweet love
making - THATS LOVE -
you know, when your
arguing all day, and time is
getting late,

Y'all can still lay in the bed
and cuddle the night away
THATS LOVE -
you know, when your man
gives you flowers for no
reason
kisses you while you're
sleeping, holds you when
your weeping, and
listens when your venting.
-NOW THAT'S LOVE!

23

MEMORY OF PAIN

WHAT?
You think you know pain?
Naw I mean you looking at
me like you know how I
feel and you feel the same...
So I ask again
You think you know pain?
Do you know how it feels
to have a smile on your
face but at the same time
feel as if all your emotions
been drained?
Have you witness
excruciating cries and
screams as you stood and
watched
too young to put up a fight

only 9 the new self-
proclaimed man of the
house since the man who's
is not a man who fathered
you ran out? Huh
Have you had dreams that
quickly turned into
nightmares
that made ya believe at any
moment of joy can become
a part of your fear, damn;
Now at 22 still can't help to
believe it was still my fault
As if I allowed it to happen
because I was torn between
two that I loved.
To the teenage girl it
happened to,
I'm sorry!
From the bottom of my
heart and soul and I
promise I would die before
that happens again.

Spoken Word

To the man who is not a
man who did it
I for gave but did not
forget.
I have suppressed the
frequent thoughts of it, but
still see
So To the man who is not a
man
GOD will have the finally
say and as you walk free
your soul will forever be a
prisoner and slower rot
To the man who is not a
man who fathered me
FUCK YOU, WE STILL
LIVE
With our heads up despite
all the pain you have
caused we still live;
Despite YOU!
So I ask again you think
you know pain?

U have no idea!

Ramon Bonner

NO TIME
TO LOVE

Love knows no time
love at first sight could be
love for life
even though it was just
your beauty and
we didn't go to a dinner
and a movie
we didn't get trapped by
making a baby
we didn't take years to
realize we should be more
than friends
in a matter of minutes, no
second, in a blink of an eye
by your walk
by your smile
by your voice made me

realize
you the one I wanted
the one I needed in my life

26

NOTHING SEXUAL

I'm going to seduce you
baby girl with my words
and my mind
I don't need to touch your
body or kiss you slowly
down your spine
We'll fall in love with a
connection by our eyes
I'll take it slow before I let
you see what I have
between my thighs
Patience is a virtue but I
don't feel that I'm wasting
time
If I want something bad
enough I'll wait until the
end of the world until its
mine

Understand my world lights
up by you when you smile
Just the thought of you
picks me up when I am
down
For twenty-two years I've
been searching but came up
empty
I'm in a world full of gold
diggers
More liars and more hoes in
which this world has plenty
I'm telling you this man
right here
With his heart on his sleeve
There is only one woman
for me and that woman is
you
Sweet lady my sweet lady
once we meet I promise
There will be nothing but
the sky above you

QUESTIONS

Have you ever had any man
like you just for you?
In every way possible,
didn't want you to change
anything about you?
Liked you for your flaws
just as much as your
positives?
Just wanted to hold you as
long as you needed at every
ounce of sadness that you
showed?
Have you ever had a man
that just by your touch
Made him feel like he don't
need anything or anyone
else but you?
Have you ever had a man
that would give you his last
breath if he knew it would
keep you alive?
These questions are for you
to let you know that you
have had and do have that
man and will always have
him with me?

Cherish what's in front of
you instead of what's
behind you or haven't came
yet!!

RELATIONSHIPS

You hate me? Really?
I'm dead to you now huh?
Really?
After all we been through, I
mean not talking about
what we going through
right now
But everything before that,
really?
You can just bring yourself
to look me in my eyes
despite the pain and tears,
yes real men do cry
although showing emotions
is our biggest fear;
and tell me we're done?
When you were distressed,
Who held you with your
head on their chest until
you fell asleep?
With a single wipe who
dried your tears as they fell
from your misty eyes
as they hit your cheeks
but you hate me now right?
Did you hate me when
money was low but
I still found a way to make
a beautiful candle light
dinner when you got off
work huh? Did you hate me
then?
How about when your
weight wasn't your weight
and you asked if you was
still pretty
I said no, you are not. I then
went on to tell you that you
are beyond pretty
In fact, you are even more
beautiful than the first time
our eyes met,

that you are more beautiful
than one mind can create,
that you are not pretty but
as a matter of fact you are
the definition of true
beauty! But you hate me
now, don't you?
Did I, despite you saying
I'm not worth shit at times,
did I say I hate you?
No actually, I said I love
you,
because in that moment I
realized that I am not
perfect,
I realize my imperfections
were only perfections and
they made me who I am in
your eyes. So can I bring
myself to utter the words I
hate you?
No, I can't. Although the
words "I hate you" hurt all

on its own,
you saying them hurts
worse,
for the simple fact that no
matter what we've been or
are going through
I do, and always will, love
you; but you hate me and
by you speaking them
words, tell me you are no
longer meant for me!

Bring yourself to realize
and understand that what
you have is what you have
and when it's gone, it's
gone for good!

SELFWORTH

In the time of descent, self
determination should never
quit
Know that your mind and
will far surpasses the
negativity of those around
you
In order for your enemies to
win, it would mean that you
as self allowed them to kill
your determination and
suppress your heart of the
very thing it is that you
love to do
Be who you are and do that
to the best of your ability
You know what it is that
makes you great at the
thing you do
You! Know what it is you
have to offer
YOU! Know once given
that fair opportunity
THEY will see and know
what it is they need!

SHOW MY LOVE

The things I speak are more
than just words
The things I think are
thought never had
The things I write are more
than just ink on a pad
When I feel, I feel from
deep down, because that's
the only place its real
So touch your hand to
mines
Let our mouths speak
nothing
Let my eyes grab your soul,
and let our hearts intertwine
I'll love less of your body
and love more of your mind

The first moment I see you,
I'll tell you that your more
beautiful than last time
So when I speak your name
it's much more than just
that
When I think about you, I
in vision what you mean to
me
When I write a love poem, I
write it with apart of you in
every line
What I feel for you.....
What I feel for
you....man...what I feel for
you
I can't put in words, I can
only mime!

Skin

From birth you wore it
as a kid you showed it
as a teen you grew self
conscious of it
as an adult you embraced it
your body your skin I love
it
The look
The scent
The feel
The taste of it
your body, your skin I love
it
You are your skin and body
and I love every inch of the
body and skin you're in

SUICIDE LETTER

Dear whom it my concern,
I sit here on my bed
reminiscing in my head
about everything I've done
and things I have yet did
(Ha) you know it's funny
though, when your little
you long to be older
when you grow up you
wish you were young
Being young is when you
have no worries
You're not supposed to do
anything but be happy and
play;
Were you that child that
was going through
depression?
Juggling with every
emotion? Asking yourself
why you don't fit in
even with your fake laugh
and grin
Everything about you was
often a joke to everybody
Either you were to skinny
so everybody always made
something relating to being
skinny rhyme with your
name
you were too fat so
everything pertaining to
you dealt with you being
hungry or tired
(Yeah), and children are
supposed to always be
happy, damn cruel world
huh!? Even going through
that as a child, that still
wasn't the breaking point

Now I'm nothing more than
just a simple teenager
Maybe life will be easier
for me, maybe depression
was just phase
(Ha) you'll like to think so
huh? You often ask
yourself "what's wrong
with me" when you see all
your friends coupled up but
you
So many clicks to belong to
in high school but you
never want to be that dude
no that fool who sneaks off
to the bathroom to
conversate with another
dude who looks like,
sounds like, and stands
alone like you because the
so called best and worst
clicks didn't want you
So you play sports thinking

it would get the frustrations
about life out but you're out
shined by someone who
doesn't have the heart for it
like you do They, with all
the talent in the world but
don't care about playing
They who plays because
their parents made them
Life sucks huh?
Now I'm bending but
haven't broken yet and I've
just been approached by the
real world
Bills, cut off notices, no job
and lonely; and it's only the
beginning. Everything you
try never seems to work
the constant failure just
brings hurt
You're grown and back at
you parents as if time
seemed to go backwards

Ramon Bonner

This is the breaking point!
This is as far as I go!
I'm sorry to my love ones,
something's you just can't
understand
no matter how much you
saying you do, makes you
think it's helping;
It doesn't! I'm done
fighting back tears in the
mean time, and shedding
tears in my spare time, to
only fall asleep and wake
up to the same pain, hurt,
depressing feelings all over
again
So once again I'm sorry
I just need to be numb to it
all
I need to know how not to
hurt anymore!
I just want to be free!
So don't be sad when I'm

gone, no tears needed to be
shed as you over see them
lay my head
Just know now I don't hurt
Just know now I'm at
peace!
Love you and always will
be in your hearts!

As you think about what
you just read; understand
that there are people out
there right now, as we
speak that is thinking like
this. Some of those people
are close and in your
family. Don't let them walk
alone! LOVE!

*Dedicated to O.J. Murdock
& Kevin Duke*

THE ORIGINAL

There's nothing like the
original
To have
To hold
To kiss
In life there comes
duplicates
That walk, talk, and smell
like the original
To the naked eye you
would swear it was true
To the one that cares
The one who dreams would
know the differences
between the two
There nothing like the
original

To HAVE
TO HOLD
TO KISS.
THERES NOTHING LIKE
THE ORIGINAL
CAUSE THERE'S NO
ONE LIKE YOU!

TRAPPED IN THE DARKNESS

Trapped in the darkness all
your life
Until darkness is all you
know until you come to
light
The pain and suffering
seems to grow
The hurt and the bad fails
to go
A touch from a love one
could calm the nerves
When the darkness clears
and the mist has vanish
The emotions builds up
Nerves get shocked
Your eyes full up to where
there's no more room to
hold tears
You call for someone no
answer
You call for your mother
but still no answer
You call for all your closest
love ones
but your calls
 Went unanswered
All your calls except for
one!
Trap in the darkness all
your life
You couldn't see who
really cared
You reached out your hand
For someone
The one who reached back
Pulled you to light
You didn't know was there
Now No longer trapped in
the darkness

Spoken Word

But through the light is
where you appear
You let the fear die down
All the tears drain away!
You are no longer trapped
in the terrible black of
darkness

Now you're carried by
lovely rays of light!
Never give up on what
you're looking for!!

TROUBLED SOME

Troubled some
I'm just a troubled soul
Trying to find my way
home
can't help feeling like I lost
my mind ever since you left
me alone
(Sing)Troublesome
I'll sing to you baby
(Sing)I am just a troubled
soul
Sometimes I let my anger
get the best of me
It's as if I always thought
you were testing me
Trying to see if I would put
my hands on you

Girl I'm in love with you
Can't you tell my love is
true
I'll go to the end of the
world for you
Don't doubt me baby
My heart beats for you
Let's be honest
I know I messed up
The hurt won't let up
Just don't give up
We can make this work
Let's just make up
Not just cover up
The situation cause the
humiliation would keep
knocking until you blow up
Damn I fucked up
I hope I luck up
And see you when I lift my
head up!.
I love you girl and I'm
sorry! True love

TRUE LOVE

I need love,
LL bumbing in the
headphones
I love strong
My hearts empty cause she
loved wrong
I close my eyes but I can't
sleep
I cook food but I can't eat
Fighting back tears so I
can't blink
What do you have left if
you gave your all
Do you stay and fight even
when your strength is gone
It cut deep, bleed now but
not for long
Keep moving forward or
your broken heart won't

fail to mend wrong

Love hurts but you got to
give 110
Love fades all but once;
true loves stay at the end

WAR

We are at war!
Some say if you start strong
you'll finish out on top
Which is true in most cases,
but this war!
This war that we're in,
consists of battles:
Battles of which a slight
slip or simple overlook can
end the complete war
In this war its all about
strategies
You should start with a
strategy
Maintain a strategy
Continue to build a strategy
to only strengthen the
chemistry between your
team

No matter what, you have
to protect what you have
You got to be careful of
traps
Outsiders that's always
trying to take what's yours
Always stand your ground
never let your weakness be
shown
A battle can be lost at any
moment, but the war can
still be saved
It depends on how bad do
you want it, how fast can
you recover
Do you want to save what
is left or do you want to
Throw in the towel?
Remember battles can
always be recovered from
Once the war is over the
war is lost forever!
This war is called love! The

Spoken Word

Battles are: the first hello,
Dating, Moving in together,
And marriage!
All can be recovered from,
But love is what holds them
together!

WHAT CAN

What can make a woman
weak
What can make a woman
weep
Could it be the way that she
is touched?
Could it be a soft kiss from
love?
What can make a woman
lose her speech?
What can knock a woman
off of her feet?
Stuck in the moment of
love and lust until she
gasping to breathe
Windows and mirrors
fogged to where no one can
see!
I can be that!

I will do that!
I can be what knocks you
off your feet
Then I'll love you forever!

WHAT DOES THIS WORLD HAVE FOR ME

What does this world have
for me?
What is my destiny?
Through the mirror I look
at me, I never see the good
just the same thing as my
enemies
I'm at a dead end down a
one way, no crossroads just
blind faith
Here I stand, yes I am, from
a boy to a man I understood
and understand

that nothing that is worth
having in this hateful;
pain forsaken world is free
You may be misguided
along your path to whatever
it is the world has in store
for you
You may feel worthless to
the point where you
question the very meaning
of your existence
For ever dark corner there's
a lighted alley
For every closed door, two
or more opens
Although you as self can't
see the admirable of your
presence, and
accomplishments
Does not mean they go
unnoticed!

Do for self before you set

out to please anyone else!
One's accomplishments
can't truly be meaningful
unless they are
acknowledged by that of
self first!

WHAT I WISH FOR

I want just one woman I
can give all my love to
Just as my heart beats for
me
My love flows for you
No more games, no lies,
just true faith, true love
between us two
No I'm not perfect and
neither will she
For who I'm looking for I
will make her feel better
than perfect
In which her heart will see
So give me your hand
I'll give you my heart
Care for mines as I will

yours and ill promise
nothing or no one in this
world will tear us apart!

WHAT I WISH FOR PT.2

I look for a woman who's
mind I can respect
A woman who's on a whole
different level when it
comes to intellect!
The first thing I think about
is not sex
The last thing to come to
mind is not how wet!
My age might be young but
my mind and soul has
surpassed my number
A kiss on the first date
would be the highlight for
days
Take time to learn
something about each other
Something more than just a
name
Everybody can be a one
night stand
At the end of it all
I would like to be a one
woman man!

Be a respectable man
before you look for a
respectable woman!

WHAT IS PERFECTION TO YOU

Judge me not by my tattoos
As for the truth lies in the
ink that intertwine with my
skin which tells a story
that's true
Judge me not by the clothes
I wear
For those naive and closed
minded people; this may be
all I have
Judge me not by the race of
my skin
For nobody chose the color
of their skin
They only have a choice to
embrace it

The way you view a person
is the same way someone
else will view you
In a world built by people
imperfections
The will to be perfect will
ultimately kill self keeping
thy from perfection!

Judge me not and I shall
not judge them!
Be who you are for you!

WHERE I CAME FROM

How is it that you have power over me?
Did I allow this to happen?
Do I not have a mind in which I can think, or a mouth in which I can speak, I know I do not walk this path alone, but this metal against my skin the colder it gets as each day begins.
Why do I, as a man, do I not deserve respect? It states that every man is created equal, but as we are paraded around like animals with these slashes on our backs as acts of disobedience
It's as if they think they're above GOD!; WRONG!
I am of all sound, mind, body and soul
However there are just some things in which a person cannot control
As time passes
The feel of cold metal on my skin is no more
I now walk alone but with a crowd behind me
Nay say to the nay Sayers that say get over it slavery ended long ago
They're right
Although we are no longer "chain chain the linked up gang"
The pigmentation of our

skin still don't allow us to
do some thing's
No, no this is not an "old
Negro spiritual" or a " we
are the world" this is more
of an outlook on where we
are and where we been
Understand we do not
always have oversight of
what we go through
With that being said,
we do always have a choice
in where we go through life
Today I can be proud and
say "I know where I came
from, and I know where
I'm going.
Today I can say "thank you
to my ancestor for their
struggle"
For them I'm here!

WRITE YOUR OWN STORY

I must not give into defeat
from anyone
For I am my own success
story
Deliver me from the evils
that surround me in this
world
For I am my own success
story
The battles that I have
faced
The pains and downs I have
surpassed
I have left them in
yesterday and made it to
today
For I am my own success
story
At the end of my story
GOD will be the final critic
Until my book ends
I'll live life, and let the man
in the mirror be my only
narrator
My destiny is mine to
create
For I am my own success
story!
Do the impossible, except
no limitations!

YOUR LAST DAY

If you woke up this
morning and today was
your last
would you cherish what
you have or think back to
what you had
if you woke up this
morning and today was
your last
would you want to see
again the love from your
past or would you be happy
with the one that lasted
if you woke up this
morning and today was
your last

would you try to see the
world or spend the day with
your love

if I woke up this morning
and today was my last
I would look to my side and
love what I have
if I woke up this morning
and today was my last
you're my past
my present and my future
so I wouldn't have to look
back again
if I woke up this morning
and today was my last
I would be happy where I
was at, seeing what I were
seeing because you are my
world

Ramon Bonner

ABOUT THE AUTHOR

Born in 1989, Ramon Bonner has always had a love for sports; football mainly. He has had a rollercoaster of a ride in his football career due to injuries. Always a pretty shy person, never a man of many words; he often did not know how to express emotions or feelings. Through trials and tribulations, heart brakes, and death of loves ones; in his late teens, Ramon begun to find a way to speak from his heart without having to speak at all. Today he has a new found love in his poetry. He has found away to transform his heart and soul into words that talk louder than any one person could ever speak